6.90

JULIAN MAY

WHY PEOPLE ARE DIFFERENT COLORS

Illustrated by
SYMEON SHIMIN

HOLIDAY HOUSE • NEW YORK

FOREWORD

The topic of race stirs more controversy today than perhaps any other area of anthropology. There is no agreement upon the number of races; many scientists acknowledge the five described in this book—while others subdivide mankind into as many as 60 racial populations. A few scientists state that there is no such thing as race at all, maintaining that the study of human differences merely serves to perpetuate prejudice. The author believes that it is futile to deny that different types of human beings exist. The study of adaptive changes in the human body is as fascinating as any other area of life science and need not be ignored. An understanding of the reasons why people of many colors exist will help us achieve a genuine brotherhood among men.

Men come in many colors. In North America today,
there are people with tan or reddish skins,
straight black hair, and narrow eyes.

There are also people with skins of brown and black,
who have tightly curled black hair.

And there are also people with pinkish-white or olive skins, whose hair may be straight or curly, and colored blond, brown, red, or black.

All of these different people live together in our land.
They are all part of the family of man—what scientists
call the human species. The different colors of hair and skin
show that long ago relatives of today's people
lived in different parts of the world.

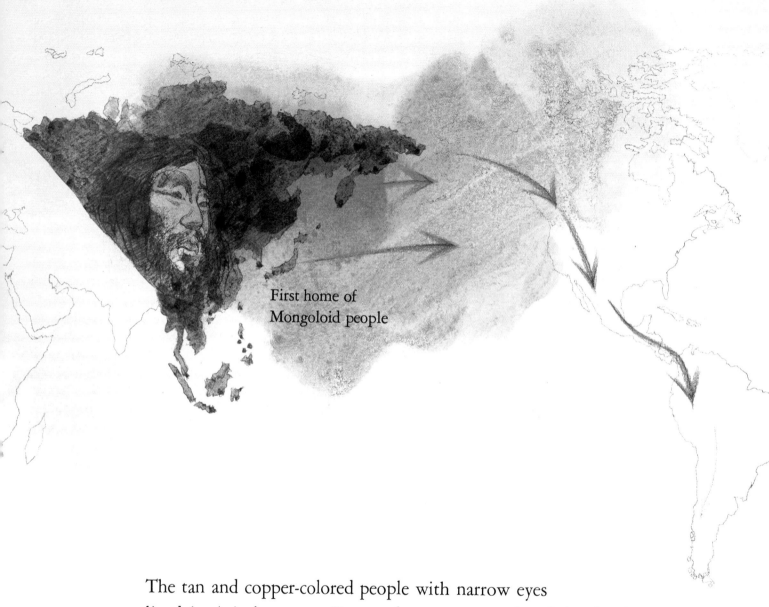

First home of
Mongoloid people

The tan and copper-colored people with narrow eyes
lived in Asia long ago. Even today, many people of this kind
live there. These people are called Mongoloid (*mon*-gull-oyd).

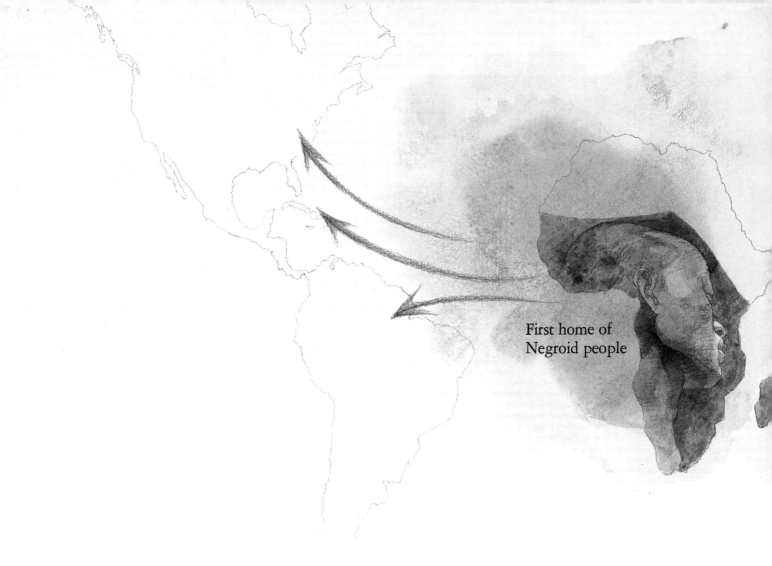

First home of
Negroid people

The black and brown people with tightly curled hair
lived in Africa long ago, and many African people
of today still look like this. These people
are called Negroid (*nee*-groyd).

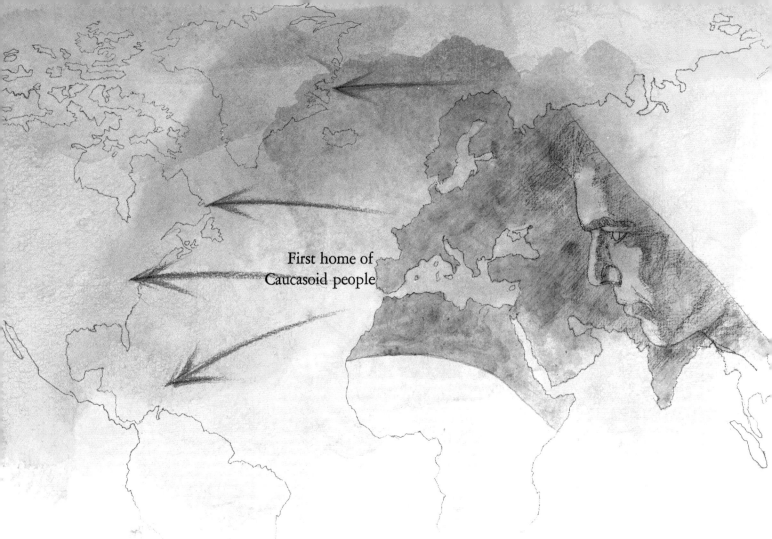

First home of
Caucasoid people

The pinkish-white and olive people with different-colored hair
all lived in Europe or northern Africa or western Asia
long ago. And many people of this kind still live there today.
These people are called Caucasoid (*kaw*-kuh-zoyd).

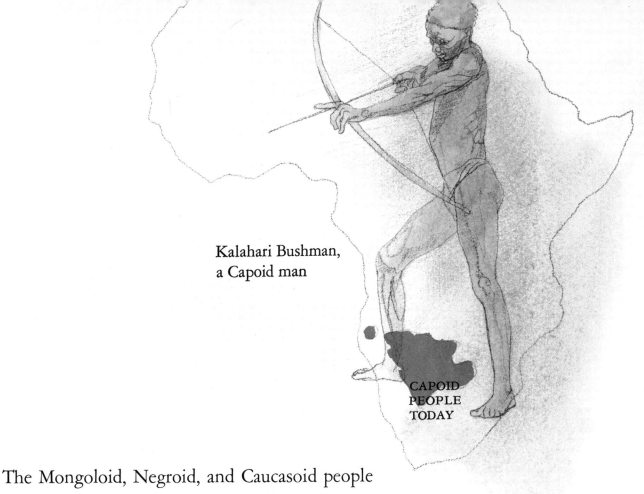

Kalahari Bushman,
a Capoid man

CAPOID
PEOPLE
TODAY

The Mongoloid, Negroid, and Caucasoid people
form three great groups, or races, of mankind.
Besides these three, there are two other, smaller, races.
The Capoid (*kay*-poid) people have yellow-tan skins,
very tightly curled black hair, and narrow eyes.
Today they live mostly in South Africa.

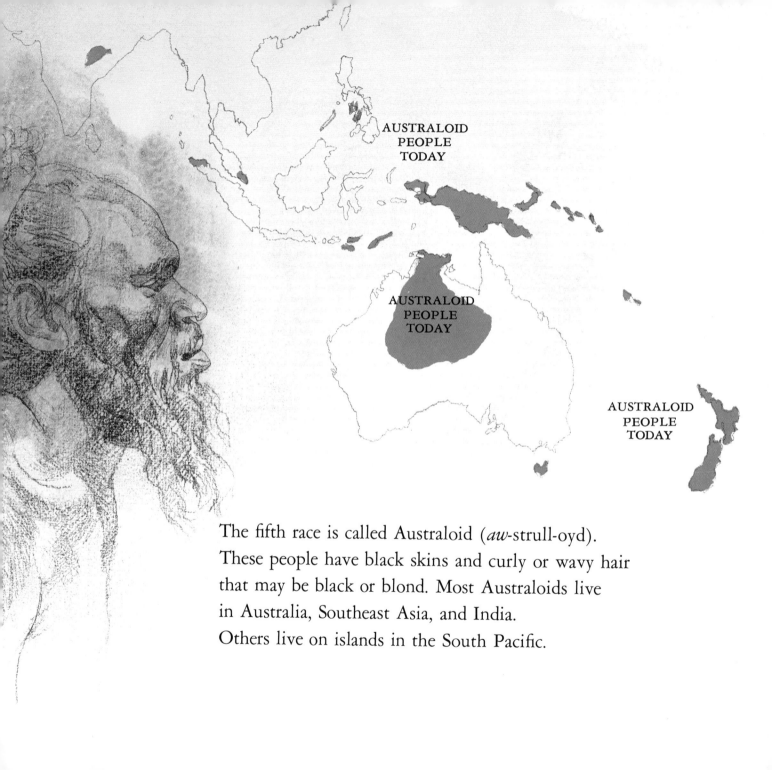

AUSTRALOID
PEOPLE
TODAY

AUSTRALOID
PEOPLE
TODAY

AUSTRALOID
PEOPLE
TODAY

The fifth race is called Australoid (*aw*-strull-oyd).
These people have black skins and curly or wavy hair
that may be black or blond. Most Australoids live
in Australia, Southeast Asia, and India.
Others live on islands in the South Pacific.

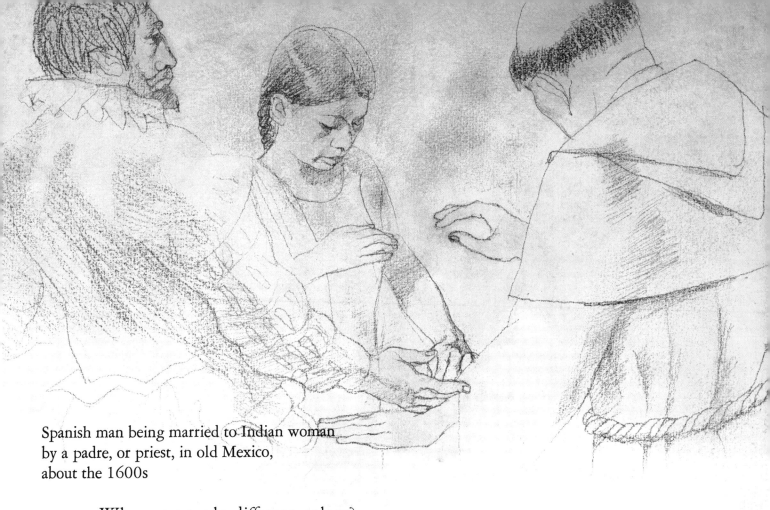

Spanish man being married to Indian woman
by a padre, or priest, in old Mexico,
about the 1600s

Why are people different colors?
This question has been asked ever since the time
that the first explorers began to travel from Europe to distant lands.
Often these men took women of other colors to be their wives.
Children of all colors were born. No matter what color
a person is, he is still part of the human family.

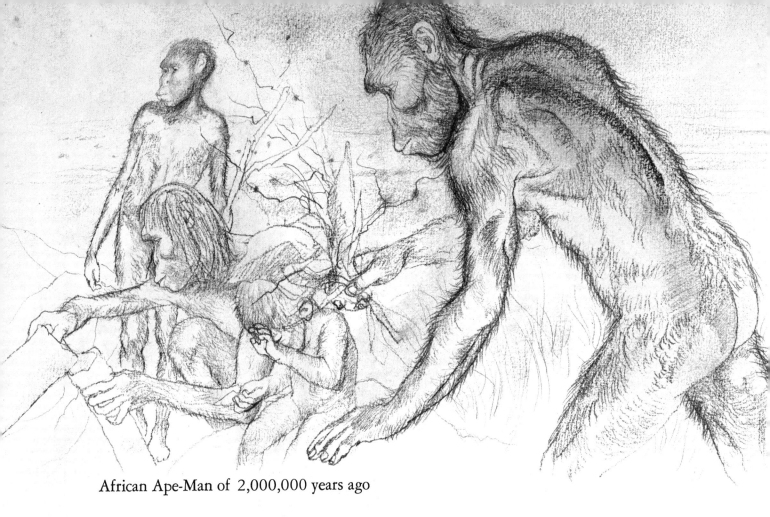

African Ape-Man of 2,000,000 years ago

There is much that is uncertain about why people are
different colors. But here are some things that are known
about the different races of mankind. First—the human
species is very old. The first real men lived in Africa
more than two million years ago. No one knows
what color they were.

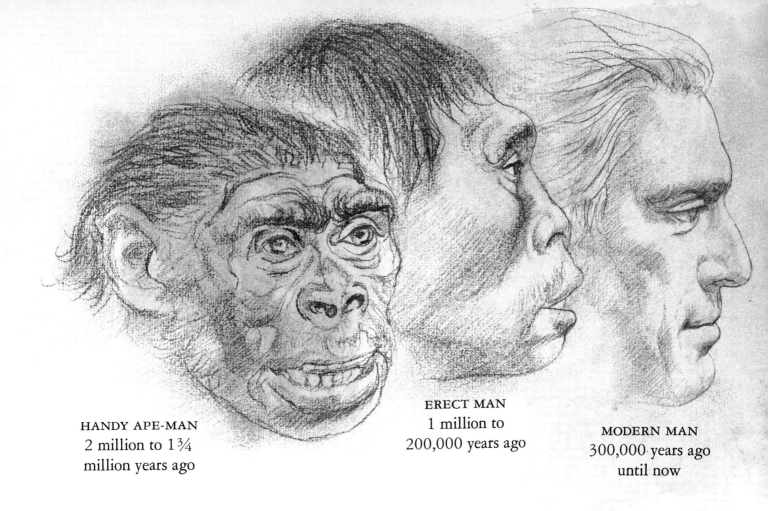

HANDY APE-MAN
2 million to 1¾
million years ago

ERECT MAN
1 million to
200,000 years ago

MODERN MAN
300,000 years ago
until now

These early men had brains only one-third as large as those
of today's men. Through thousands of years, man's brain slowly became larger.
And the rest of man's body changed, or evolved, too.
The "modern" type of man began to live on earth nearly 300,000
years ago.

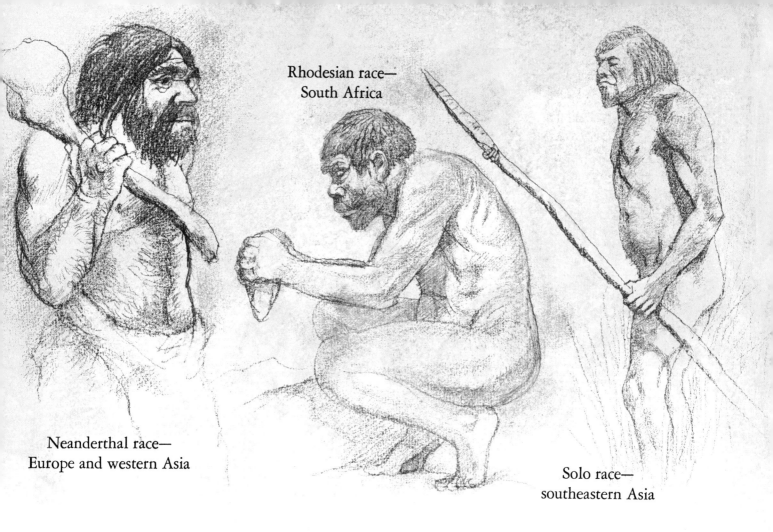

Rhodesian race—
South Africa

Neanderthal race—
Europe and western Asia

Solo race—
southeastern Asia

The first races of modern people looked something like these pictures.
Nobody knows what color they were.
These people may look strange to us, but
they could think and make tools. Their brains
were just about as large as ours.

The Cro-Magnon people were Ice Age
hunters more than 30,000 years ago

As thousands of years passed, new races appeared
in certain places. The Cro-Magnon race came from the Middle East
to Europe. They are thought to be the ancestors
of today's Caucasoid race. But scientists do not agree
about the ancestors of the other modern races.

Anthropologists at work

Scientists who study the races of mankind are called
anthropologists. Among the things they study are man's hair,
his skin color, the shape of his face, and the shape of his body.
These things help to show where a person's ancestors came from.

Anthropologists believe that body differences once helped
men to live in different climates. Perhaps the thick,
wavy hair of Caucasoids was once a protection from the chilly,
rainy climate. The straight hair of Mongoloids is
an even better protection against the cold.

Negroid people on the veldt, or grassland

Negroid and Capoid people have a special kind of very curly hair.
It grows thickly and seems to protect the head
from very hot sun. It took thousands and thousands
of years for different types of hair to become
the way they are now.

Australoid children often have blond hair
that turns dark later

Caucasoids have the most hair colors—black, brown, red, blond,
and all colors in between. The other races have mostly
black hair that sometimes turns white in old age.
The color of hair does not seem to harm or help
a race much in its way of life.

The Ainu people, Caucasoids of Japan, are the hairiest
people on earth today. One ancient custom, tattooing
women's lips, is dying out

It seems likely that the earliest people on earth had
very hairy bodies. Does this mean that today's hairiest races
are the oldest? Perhaps. Caucasoids have the most body hair,
followed by Australoids. Capoids have more body hair
than Negroids—and the Mongoloids have the least of all.

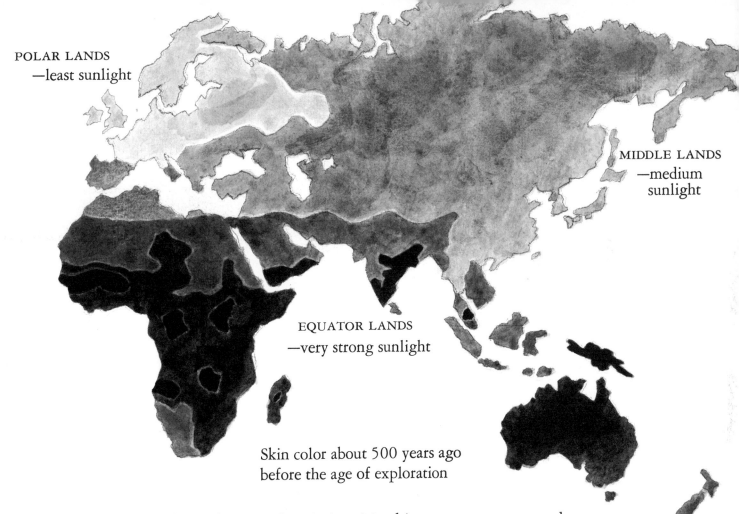

POLAR LANDS
—least sunlight

MIDDLE LANDS
—medium
sunlight

EQUATOR LANDS
—very strong sunlight

Skin color about 500 years ago
before the age of exploration

As man's body became less hairy, his skin was more exposed
to the sun. Its color became important. Special light rays
from the sun act on the skin to make vitamin D,
which is needed for the growth of people's bodies.
Too much of this vitamin is harmful;
and too much sunlight can also cause sunburn.

DARK NEGROID
OF AFRICA

DARK CAUCASOID
OF INDIA

DARK AUSTRALOID
OF NEW GUINEA

About 500 years ago, before people began
moving all over the world, the darkest-skinned
people lived nearest the equator. This is
the sunniest place. Their dark skins helped
protect them from sunburn and from getting too
much vitamin D.

Light-skinned Scandinavians live
in a cloudy climate with dark winters

But people living in cloudier lands did not need
dark skins. Lighter skins are needed where sunlight is weak,
so that the body can make enough vitamin D to stay healthy.
There were two Ice Ages, with cloudy skies, during
the 300,000 years that modern man has lived.
So it seems that some people must have become
light-skinned a long time ago.

Look again at the skin-color map a few pages back.
The equator line shows where the sun is
brightest. But skin color does not grow
slowly lighter and lighter as one moves
north or south of the equator. Instead,
there are "patches" of different-colored
people. This happened because large groups
having a certain skin color slowly moved
away from their first homes to new places.
In many parts of the world, people of
different colors lived together. After many
years, their children looked somewhat like
one race and somewhat like another. Even
today, some people—such as the Polynesians—
are not easily placed in any one race group.

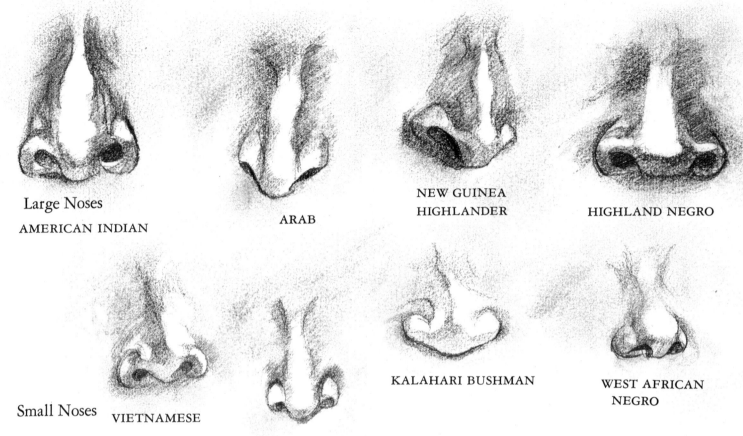

Large Noses
AMERICAN INDIAN

ARAB

NEW GUINEA
HIGHLANDER

HIGHLAND NEGRO

Small Noses   VIETNAMESE

PHILIPPINE NEGRITO

KALAHARI BUSHMAN

WEST AFRICAN
NEGRO

The shape of the face is another thing studied by anthropologists.
People have different-shaped noses. No one knows
exactly why. The nose warms and moistens air
before it reaches the lungs, and people in cold
or dry places often have the largest and longest noses.

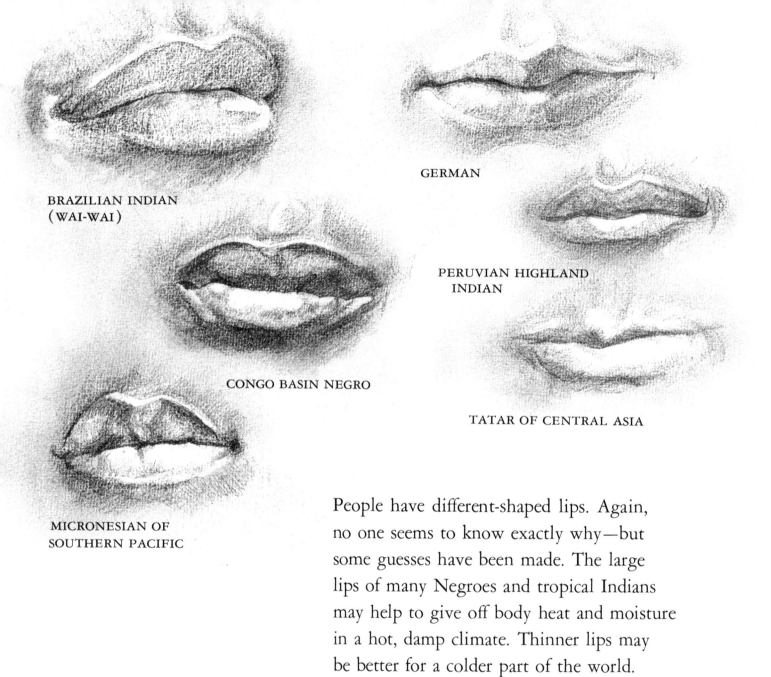

BRAZILIAN INDIAN
(WAI-WAI)

GERMAN

PERUVIAN HIGHLAND
INDIAN

CONGO BASIN NEGRO

TATAR OF CENTRAL ASIA

MICRONESIAN OF
SOUTHERN PACIFIC

People have different-shaped lips. Again,
no one seems to know exactly why—but
some guesses have been made. The large
lips of many Negroes and tropical Indians
may help to give off body heat and moisture
in a hot, damp climate. Thinner lips may
be better for a colder part of the world.

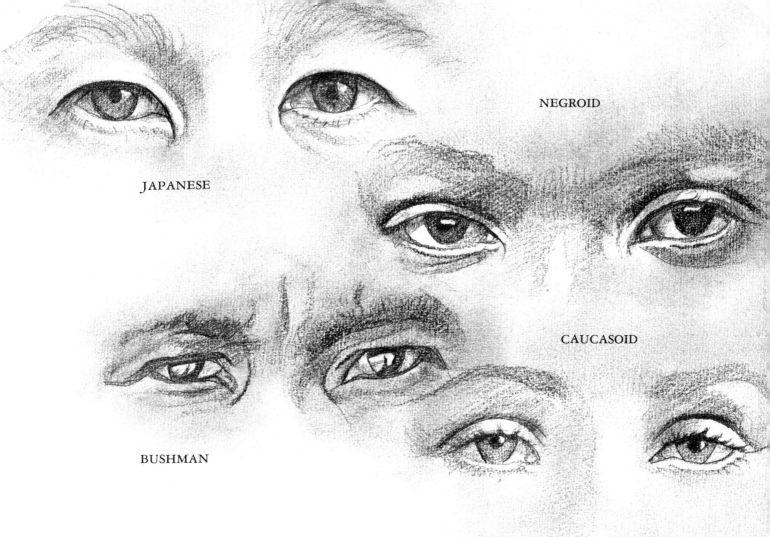

JAPANESE

NEGROID

CAUCASOID

BUSHMAN

In Mongoloid and Capoid people, the eyelid has
a fold of skin that makes the eye look narrow
or "slanted." Some Mongoloid eyes are much narrower
than others.

Naga tribe,
India and Burma

Iroquois tribe,
eastern North America

"EARLY" MONGOLOID PEOPLES

Kwakiutl tribe,
Pacific coast of
North America

Many anthropologists believe that the Mongoloids
with the least "slanted" eyes are the oldest branch
of their race. These would include the American Indians,
who came from Asia perhaps 40,000 years ago.
Perhaps these "early" Mongoloids developed from Caucasoids
or Australoids long ago.

MALAY

GREENLAND ESKIMO

MONGOL

The "newer" Mongoloids include the Eskimos and many people
of Asia. Their eyes look narrow because there are folds of skin
around them. It is thought that these people first lived
in a very cold part of Northern Asia, where such eyefolds
would protect against freezing. Later the "new" Mongoloids
moved southward and eastward.

Differences in body size in Negroids

TUTSI TRIBE
OF AFRICA

AMERICAN NEGRO
OF U.S.A.

PYGMY
OF AFRICA

Body and head size are also studied by anthropologists.
All races have some members who are tall, some who are medium,
and some who are short. And all races have
some people with larger brains and some with smaller.

Long ago, when race differences first developed,
people lived lives much different from ours today.
They stayed outside a lot. The color of their skins,
their hair type, the shape of their faces,
and other body differences helped them stay alive
in their particular part of the world.

Today, race differences do not help us
so much in our lives. Body color and hair type
are not important when one wears clothes
and a hat and does not have to live outdoors
in very hot or very cold weather. But it
is interesting to learn how race differences
developed, and why people are different colors.